thoughts from a middle-aged hag

M.E. Lanie

thoughts from a middle-aged hag
A collection of poems from M.E. Lanie
Doral, Florida, USA

Cover design by M.E. Lanie

ISBN 978-1-7360621-0-4 (paperback)
ISBN 978-1-7360621-1-1 (ebook)
ISBN 978-1-7360621-2-8 (hardback)

Library of Congress Control Number: 2020922058

Facebook, Twitter or Instagram: @laniepoetry

This is dedicated to my Mom, Dad and sister, who have been so encouraging and supportive throughout the journey of getting this book published.

Content

my fire still burns
bright

keep at it. (158)

stand
and, shout
let others hear
about the dysfunction
of what we hold dear

don't
back down
when they distract
with false words
and, masked attacks

call
on others
to take a side
for their silence is loud
heartbreaking, can't deny

here to stay. (27)

boom boom
pit pit patter
we know what matters
for we won't go tonight
not 'til wrongs are made right
and, we speak the facts
so, don't do us like that

tap tap
zip zip zap
you know where it's at
we're the leaders of what is to be
yet, you're not listening to our homily
but that's okay, you know
because we're about to take over the show

we the persons. (13)

it's lovely to be
the one who openly
discusses the things that don't feel right
lest we forgot our numbers and might
many of us hide
because of the tide
that lately goes where darkness grows
but, remember that lunar light tows
and, ebbs will follow
to a place hallowed
by the goodness that remains
within you, me and the sane
for then we will see
there's more to me
and, to you and everyone who
stand for the red, white and blue
than what divides
so, let's not fight
with our brothers and sisters
and, neighbors and misters
for one day
love will slay
and, we will all wonder
how we came to be sundered
saying we will
never be ill
to one another again
here's hoping, amen

dear john. (12)

lies, lies, lies
you just deny
never take the side
of those in the right
you gots to know your words divide
the hate you fuel may never subside
you amplify from the pot
then abandon us to rot
in this tension you orchestrated

unity. (96)

be gone
from this place
we will
congregate
to unite
and, celebrate

future. (107)

the outlook is bleak
there's not much we can retrieve
but, we have one another
and, our right to believe

continue. (125)

we'll build this
you and i
despite the stares of passerbys
for they aren't believers of what can be
but, you and i see beyond the trees

just remember
all will fall in place one day
as long as we continue this pace

soldier on. (176)

in the midst of chaos
in the realm of isolation
we must look past
this timeline of desperation
for our victory is beyond the horizon
though, it will elude us
unless we acknowledge this isn't our zion

got you. (62)

your pain
is not my pain
your plight
isn't mine
i'll never see through your eyes
that's a fact of life

but, i see you
i hear you
i feel you
so, i've made the choice
to be your voice
and, one day
i'll ask you to do the same
to help alleviate my pain

hide. (130)

culture is no excuse
for ignorant views
or, shelling out abuse

just read the room
to note how much we grew
and, think about how you
can change your tune

disrupt. (127)

the prince calls upon us to do his bidding
though, we commoners are now thinking
the status quo never did us any good
so, we're pondering if we should even groove
we stare back at him with reluctant eyes
but, he already knows the direction of the tide

happy days are here. (147)

i woke this morning in utter disbelief
you had warned of a reckoning
a correction, at least
but, all i see is the sun shining once more
and, a rumbling beyond my door

reach out. (57)

my time with you
should help me think anew
but, all i can see
is how backwards you can be
and, how you don't embrace
those with a different face
that's just too much
and, it brings me disgust
so, sorry to say
i'll be walking that way

pervasive angst

becoming you. (21)

i hear rumors that in the past
you were an independent kick ass
with beauty and beaus amassed
what brought you to this impasse?

oh, white witch, you scare me so
walking to your empty home
with your crumpled bags in tow
and, your whispers to your own

i am so obsessed, you see
because i will become you, undoubtedly

helpless. (69)

oh, why do i continue
to play this game
the odds are against me
i can't spin it my way
i'm drowning
in this mess
i have to find a way out
or else, i confess,
i may burst
and, bleed out

knots. (91)

that feeling in the pit of my tummy
won't go away
the fear, the doubt, the endless dismay
it eats at my core, keeps me up at night
diminishing my might

i freeze at the thought of what's ahead
please, tomorrow, take to bed
i need a moment to think ahead

please. (79)

i just need a break
from all the hate
and, drown in nonsense
so, i can forget that we live in a mess

november. (8)

where are we going?
the tea leaves are flowing
saying there's no going back
to the time we were intact
the years we're about to embark
will bring us further apart

i feel i don't know anymore
what we are living for
all these years i stupidly thought
we had a bond as tight as a knot
now, i don't know where to go from here
and, all that we've built has disappeared

now this. (1)

a blonde can't decide
elders fuss, gents hide
in jericho, kin lament
more nonsense over precedent
quack rants, son tows
underserved voices wake xenophobes
your zen

middle ages. (26)

the growing aches
come with age
is what people say

thoughtless gaps
sometimes cause mishaps
so, don't forget to remember that

the expanding waist
will be a challenge to erase
so, you better pick up the pace

and, the lingo heard 'round town
will be confusing verbs and nouns
so, expect to feel left out

thursday night. (2)

you taunt me
with your proximity to hours free
you flirt with me
promises of bagels, mimosas and glee
you wink at me
endless hours filled with binge
you sing to me
soaking up the sun's singe
you lie to me

stress. (101)

i can't eat
i can't sleep
stress consumes me
like a viral disease
it won't go away
unless i forget my dismay
drown it in sauce
hope to give it pause

stuck. (48)

get me out of here
i don't like the atmosphere
of apathy, deflection and general bitchiness
folks not realizing how they contribute to an environment
of idleness

latina. (53)

am i me?
the being i always see
which has been turned upside down
because i'm not as authentic as those around
they're closer to the core
and, i've lived a life somewhat outside the zone

so, i have to reflect
as to what i really am
and, i don't know if i can face the results in the end

hopeless. (52)

it's gone
no more exists
with broken hearts
we're reluctant to persist
this dumpster fire
won't be extinguished
it roars on
regardless of the resistance
what happens now?

lapsang souchong. (179)

one, two
measure the scoop
three, four
let it pour
five, six
honey to mix
seven, eight
can't be late
nine, ten
won't this end?

morning. (16)

trying to get out of bed
but rather stay put instead
because life outside this castle
is just a bunch of tiresome hassle
so, i'll cut out all the chaos in between
and, stay in the place i'll end up eventually

color. (36)

you made me see my color
for until this point i was a scholar
a gen xer, an independent woman, a citizen
so many things that exist beyond this skin

now, i feel that i must choose
a side in this color feud
but, i miss the life i knew
where i was just another kid in the hood
where it didn't matter the hue
the ethnicities or the languages known too
i wasn't singled out because i'm brown
rather, i was included because i was just around

decision. (41)

it's so hard to make up my mind
i've run through the scenarios so many times
yet, i tend to think about all that could go wrong
and, then i go back to singing the same old song

denial. (73)

i see the end
it sits there staring
i try ignoring
but, i know in my pit
that i'll soon be hit
and, there's no denying
my destiny will be trying

lockdown. (138)

what have i done with all this time?
i've pondered my existence
cooked some swine

anchors gabbing day and night
think they're helping
it don't ease the fright

when will all this end?
so, that i can get back my groove
and, you can peacock once again

trapped. (180)

obsession floods my veins
through my sweat, it stains
i try to keep it at bay
but, it won't go away

why can't i just let it drop?
i want to be carefree
and, not give a fuck

catechism

prayer. (5)

who am i, but a purpose unfulfilled?
i seek your answers far and near
though, cries for visions i have still
and, now, i find myself unclear

what am i, but a she with no legacy?
as others fret and note the emptiness
i accept my fate with little hesitancy
you owe me big time, so give it up, your highness

beatitudes. (42)

and, jesus said
humility brings you home
sadness will be consoled
reward given to self control
and, justice to those who seek it most

and, jesus said
mercy will be returned
selfless ones will be blind no more
pacifists won't be disowned
and, martyrs shall make it home

eve. (54)

i was taught
that being evolved is wrong
that immersing to life outside
was acceptance of the devil
and, we would die
without the love of the guy
who made all this possible

but, then i grew up
began to drink from the kool-aid cup
and, now i see
that my learnings
were rooted deep
in fear and ignorance
an unwillingness to dance
with the unknown

remember his words. (159)

i am confused
with your words
with your insistence
with your masked sentiment
it lacks the compassion
your teacher called upon
are you sure you're a disciple?

valhalla. (14)

i dance in the streets
with moves that are exaggerated
i sing quite off beat
as musicians are recuperating
i skip through town
loving my endless pursuit
i laugh out loud
hoping that i don't puke
i cry for joy
while others reach their summits
i say a'hoy
to my maker as he cometh

it. (141)

perhaps it's missing
perhaps it's always been here
right in front of us
speaking to us
yet, we didn't want to hear

others will still deny its existence
but, a few will now see
the simplicity of it
the complexities of it
and, how it will set us free

courage. (60)

oh, why do you avoid me
when i most need you
i can't proceed
with you
you know that
but, still choose to stand back
and, i'm left on my own
heart about to blow
then, i close my eyes
internalize
and, walk

unapologetic & femme

persona. (169)

come,
take me as i am
a flawed being
a bitter ma'am

one day. (10)

i hear the thunderous march of what's to come
anticipation eats my every thought
see, the heavy shackles will come undone
a drudge vanishes, no longer a bot

for i will be free to wander far and wide
no regrets and nothing to hide
witnessing the value of my life's worth
i will be the happiest being on earth

feelings. (30)

what's in my heart today
may in some time go away
for tomorrow, i will think differently
as i process what's happening prospectively
today, i'll smile
tomorrow, i'll frown
sometimes i may be hostile
but, i rather not break down

i prefer to laugh and to love
to gossip some
be bold
be sly
take hold
a little shy
so many possibilities
from one with sensibilities

right path. (88)

i've waited this long
to join the rank and file
but, in my style
i feel so lost now
trying to disavow
this path i chose without
thinking what brings on
a fire in my song

man. (11)

man, you enter a room like you're king
it's a harsh reality for those hoping
that one day we become the powers that be
or, at least beings equal to thee

man, i see the fear growing in your eyes
because your position in our tribe
is dwindling as time goes by
and, your words are being sidelined

man, i see your attempts to chime in
along with the chorus of voices crying sin
they come for you with fire and fury
you disappear, and no one feels sorry

cuerpo. (22)

my boobs, hips and butt
physical features that summed up
are things that i cannot alter
without the scalpel from a doctor
so, i don't even bother
worrying how others
perceive me
or, believe
that the outside
mirrors the inside
for i know i am more than that
more that the body fat
more than the swollen thighs
more than the flabby sides
so, i'll just spend my time
savoring the taste of pie
tapas, yucca and wine
bacon, eggs and rice
i'll leave it to the others
to worry and bother
with the social burdens of today
that will weigh them down more than a buffet

neither here nor there. (113)

i've been to the river jordan
and, won't come back
in here, we are equals
and, don't deal with pushback

our days are our own
never prisoners to your ideas
we fear no one
so, let me make this clear
i live in the in-between
and, i prefer it here

attitude. (103)

disrespect me once
and, i'll forgive no one

adam's rib. (165)

you ask me what i am
and, i tell you i am woman first
because my sex is what causes my thirst
for when i look to have more
my gender triggers closed doors
for when i see men coast
it's their privilege that irks me the most
for when i seek to walk alone
the inquiries relate to the absent bloke

so, yes, i am woman first
i am woman now
and, i am woman forever

being. (76)

i have to believe i'm special
or, else none of this matters
the monotony, the schedules
my endless settling

it's all for a prize
am i right?
because this can drive someone mad
dealing and dealing without an end

tell me what my dreams have seen
that one day i'll be free

endless salad days. (77)

you can't deny
i am still in my prime
despite what mirrors eye
for i feel like i'm seventeen
except for the days my body screams
and, i can be progressive
just like the bed heads
don't set me aside
because i remember sly
you'll see i'll flatter
because it's mind over matter

home. (86)

i just want to go home
where things feel comfy and warm
where i know folks
and, the pace is slow
and, the air is light
and, relations are tight

duped. (136)

running, fighting, screaming
the inner workings of me
has many wondering
what will become of me

though, all their thoughts and worries
should be directed towards thee
for you are the one who's crying
deep beneath your vivid glee

reminiscing. (128)

i want to be that girl once more
the one who got to be adored
who jumped through every open door
and, didn't let fear chart her course

weddington. (177)

choice is mine
and, mine alone
no cock and balls
dare take it all

1920. (186)

you say you don't know what it's like
to live a life as a woman defined
yet, you reap the spoils of events transpired
triggered by misses who had a deep desire
to be heard
to be respected
to be counted

they wrote, screamed, and marched
sometimes beaten and detained by the oligarchs
though, they wouldn't stop
until the 19th was locked

now, we've reached the centennial mark
though, to be honest, celebrations seem a little sparse
and, now you're telling me you don't feel the part
don't you realize if it hadn't been for them
you and i wouldn't be today's woman

do it. (65)

i do it because i can
no hesitation, just waiting to see where i land

nope, don't ask where i'll be in five years
i don't do vision boards, i play it by ear

be brave. (51)

i must put on my big girl pants
and, face this world with fervor
courage
passion
eloquence
and, all i can muster
from deep within
no apologies
niceties
or, excuses
i am who i am
to the end

defeated. (64)

it doesn't matter
how long we chatter
or, how we gather
and, march as sisters
because these misters
will feel targeted and disparaged
and, will circle the wagons
to stop the stampede
of those who scream, "me!"

so, it doesn't deserve repeating
but, i fear we will be defeated

untethered. (93)

oh, how i wish this will end soon
so, that i can fly away
like a balloon
with no permanent home
just roaming the world
exploring what's known
no attachments
no distractions
just me

delusion. (89)

there's a connection
between me and perfection
it's just that you don't see
the light that's within me

reboot. (104)

can i just run away?
forget all that decay
that rots our core
and, start afresh
next time, i'll try my best

look back. (150)

yes, i took the easy way out
could've
should've
been the one who dared to stand out

now, i have some regrets
and, i retrace my steps
pondering if i should've gone left
then, i sleep and forget

knock out. (151)

this will not be my end
this will not let me down
i am strong
i am stubborn
i do not blubber
i have walked through fire
i have endured things dire
so, i get back up right now
and, others should look out

my culture. (163)

don't tell me what i am
or, how i fit into your diagram
it doesn't feel like me
and, actually offends me
because i am more complex than that

crossroads. (166)

this is supposed to be my moment
my time to shine
to bury all the naysayers
and, to make this fiefdom mine

speak. (67)

no puedo hablar
la idioma de mis padres antigua
it left me when i grew
and flew
away from those i knew

multidimensional love

knight. (106)

take me to the ball
twirl me around the mall
look in my eyes and say the words
that matter to this timid girl

repeat. (116)

i've been here before
the sounds
the smells
the bitter score

i recall very little
of you
of me
of a bond so brittle

let's try again
to learn
to love
it won't be in vain

brad. (61)

oh, go ahead and be the fun one
i'll take care of the details
while you zip along
i'll ask myself in a couple years
if i still want to be here
but, why should i wait anymore
when i know my joy is just outside that door

sweet devil. (17)

i can't stop thinking about you
how your eyes can be dark, and yet so icy blue
and, that jet black mane and bronze skin too
i've fallen for a rebellious juve

your presence drives me crazy insane
and, i can't wait 'til we meet again
but, you are the forbidden, you see
so, we can't be together openly

it's me. (7)

you're the kindest of souls
and, your warm heart is gold
any girl would be mad
to reject such a lad

yet, i struggle to see
how this works for me
i wish i could modify
that feeling i can't hide

i want the best for you
so, don't be so blue
you may hate me so
i'll take the blame and go

just remember i will be there
if you ever need someone to care

my chosen. (19)

the arts and crafts in the square
the lilies that permeate the air
the sun's warm kiss on my skin
the afternoons spent doodling
the ice tea poured with an ounce of sweet
the hot sand beneath my feet
the movies from an era gone by
the joke that lingers in my side
the waves breaking on the shore
the canine anxiously waiting at the door
the full cup of vino to unwind
the adonis so gentle and kind
the hint of sunscreen and salt to pair
the soft, frizzy head of hair
the comfort of a spanish guitar
the kinsmen both here and far
so much more to think and list
i'll finish now, but will resume, if you insist

boy crazy. (18)

i can't stop thinking about that guy
who walks around like he's so fly
it's an addiction of sorts, they say
for i have a hard time staying away

a day in the life. (23)

i loved you in the morning
when everything seemed bright, shiny and new
and, without warning
a strange feeling in my gut began to brew
around midday
i came to a realization that i saw you in a different light
as people do say
this divergence is unavoidable come twilight
as dessert is served
we are strangers sharing the same space
the moon passes
we retire wondering how we got to this place
the sun rises
we mourn what is dead
for what had begun so strong
has met its last breath

last song. (32)

are you serious about this right now?
you're leaving me for that fat cow
after all that we've been through
the good times, me and you

well, don't you dare come back
i won't be cutting you any slack
you've made your pick
so, you better hope this one sticks

missing. (178)

i seek the high of first love
it's evaded me for some time now
i look in corners and shelves above
but, it's nowhere to be found

doormat. (115)

never leave me
for i know not how to just be one
my life has always been with thee
and, you won't find another like me

i spend each day worshipping you
no matter how you soil the meaning of us two
i will continue to look the other way
because i know you love me
even though you say
the sight of me
gives you dismay

let me go. (126)

i want my name back
you at least owe me that
for i don't belong to anyone
especially to those who have come and gone

the morning after. (149)

in the light of day
i see the decay
it's something that didn't show
when the libations flowed

please get me out of here
i foresee getting some jeers

fling. (184)

let's rendezvous
under the old spruce
and, kiss away the night

it's so nice
to have a slice
of this time with you

promise me tonight
under the moonlight
that you and i will be forever

goals. (47)

at this juncture we finally meet
you're not what i expected you to be
the face, body and sound are not quite right
i anticipated someone who could put up a fight

but, i guess it's okay
that you turned out this way
for my visions never seem
to become a realization for me

microfiche

dream. (15)

words escape me now when i am about
to tell the whole wide world what's in doubt
it just won't come out
of this mouth wide open
and, my body is frozen
within this place i've chosen
to hide from those faces from my past
that were never meant to last
and, i hear their feet approaching fast
towards me
and, my lead feet
which will betray me
by forcing me to see
the eyes of those
i've left cold
and, alone

lost in my head. (175)

most days will be forgotten
names, places and things
will spill past the bottom

the recollections that stick
tell a story of who you are
and, how you think

miracle city. (20)

excuse me for the delay
i was distracted by the display
of the cutest dress at belk's
which i could use for teen town at the elk's

oh, yes, he passed me a note during p.e.
and, it basically said he's my destiny
i'm so giddy when i see him play ball
i dream of the day we marry and have it all

let's grab a soda at orange julius over there
and, i'll tell you about how she just stares
at him in every class they have together
if she gets any closer, i swear i'll belt her

let's head now to the theatre to see
the new one with the two coreys
oh, wait, look at those red heels
over at thom mcan's, and they're such a deal!

false memories. (164)

i think i remember how it was
the smells, the feel
the grandness of it all
but, when i go back
i see a tiny, old, musty shack
and, realize my perspective is at fault

january 26th. (122)

today is your birthday
it's one more day
since you've been away
and, though you're not here
the thought of you
is still very clear

i was eighteen. (33)

sometimes you drive me crazy so
with all your don'ts and no's
i feel confined by all these borders
and, how my life has all this order
just let me go free
for one day, please
i need to breathe
the air and sea
i need to escape the expectations
the judgments, rules and accusations
no one can thrive under these condemnations
don't you see the errors of this situation?

abuela. (3)

your spirit wisps over
no, no necesito un novio
my heart weighs heavy with regret
ay, déjame, no quiero comer
you left a wound to fester
si, tengo bajar de peso
your exit left a haze
dios mío, cálmate
miss you

old is not new again. (43)

i remember the very first time
the laughs, the fears, the cry
after many moons pass by
i come back for one more try
yet, the outcome isn't identical
to the experience i had a decade ago
but, it is all still the same
it's just me who has grown away

garden st. (50)

this place reminds us how fast it goes
days summed up on a bunch of stones
the quiet is cracked by the sobs
of a mother robbed of her youngest one

next door. (4)

the banging knocks and wakes
the shrill is more than i can take
yet, my little feet feel like blocks of ice
and, my intentions won't suffice
you call out a name with hope
but, i am feeling like such a dope
no help will ever come

too late. (56)

i never got the chance to thank you
let alone
bid you adieu
i've been busy with life
and everything in between
but, now i've paid the price
because you went to the beyond
without hearing the song
of how grateful i am
you were part of crafting the plan
to set me on a journey
that's taken me here, there
and everywhere
that's forced me to evolve
into a being you could've been proud of
oh, if you could've seen
how your influence affected me

me. (81)

i am meant to be great
i'm just blossoming late
you see, the gods spoke to me since days before
how i would be the one and all
i believe and have no doubts
despite the fact that little has come about
just wait and see
one day, it will be all about me

youth spent. (139)

those were happier times
times of contentment
when laughter cost a cent

little did i know
that was the end
to never dream again

i look back now
don't recognize the hue
yet, i mourn the passing of it too

don't you want to go back? (173)

i sometimes yearn for yester years
when the world wasn't dipped in fear
neighborhoods were filled with glee
and, represented an extended family
when shade was a state for relaxation
not a way to dis your relations

don't you want to turn the tide?
or, would you rather run and hide?

4717. (182)

it sits sad, empty and alone
with glass dark and broke
we whisper tales not so true
about a family that once knew
this place as house and home

they spent many years content
until the son grew despondent
parents desperately searched for clues
as to what caused his unending blues

then one dark and stormy night
while the rest of the family slept tight
the boy rummaged through the cellar
and, chose the device that would cause terror

now, i'll let your imagination explore
how the rest of this story goes
but, if you happen to hear noises next door
it's probably the ghost of that boy looking for more

mundo

nor'easter. (9)

oh, peaceful white morn, you cause such fear
folks hunkered down while all is cleared
yet, outside the silence surrounds
only interrupted when my feet pound
i savor the absence of all that is real
and, wonder why others don't greet you with zeal
stay here for longer, dear friend, i pray
your departure will leave me with such dismay

playa. (29)

water, air, salt and sand
elements that i wish were close at hand
for i have missed you much over the years
your smell, sound and feel, i have always held dear
but, i look forward to seeing you again
my dreams should suffice until then

spring. (37)

the flowers bloom
the sun floods the room
the commotion starts outside
the screen catches a fly
i sit here and ponder
how this place can be such a wonder

rainy. (35)

i walked out this morning, and it smelled like florida
outside
you know, the scent of moist, fish and salt combined
it took me back to that place
when i had a young face
and, all my worries were none too great
and, my bubble was no bigger than thirty-four square
miles
and, we had a front row seat to the starship trials

eclipse. (135)

the cheetah passes by
with speeds that turn the eye
annoyed is the woken sloth
that time must no longer be lost

family. (46)

i tried my best
to unsettle the nest
yet, nothing fell apart
because the twigs were the heart

social distance. (181)

i take off my mask
and, breathe in the fresh air
mother nature, our great savior

wise woman said

history. (31)

we continue to ignore
what's happened before
we think it's all new
but, if we just look back a few
we'd know it all happened before
and, we won't be able to again ignore

young. (39)

i do admire your idealism though
i remember when i felt the same way some time ago
that fire in the belly to make it all better
steps planned out to the letter
but, just so you know
reality can sometimes blow
so, be okay when those dreams don't come true
there might be something else in store for you

you i. (6a)

what can i say about you?
the one who lights a room
while others swoon
and, write some tunes
i lie back and sneak a snooze

what can i say about you?
the one who loves the view
you attempt a pass
and, get no lass
get out and get a clue

what can i say about you?
the one who flew the coop
you took no blame
i felt ashamed
you've taken me for a fool

ignore. (90)

there are problems out there
we'd rather not face
so, we find a place
that drowns the sound of pain
but, the shrieks of fear
will continue to come near
and, we won't be able to run
from the wrath that has begun

fantasy. (109)

dreams can cost quite a bit
they may elude you
taunt you
with visions that aren't legit

be smart. (83)

they play us like we don't matter
throw around words that clatter
bring on heat and swords
but, let's stop and breathe
and, think
that we have to be
smart or this world will sink

visionaries. (110)

the far and beyond
is concrete to no one
tellers act like they got some
but, they be unaware
of their limits, which scares
and, we keep following
like lemmings in pairs

subway rider. (34)

boy, whatcha doing over there?
you've got a lot of people scared
with your blank stare
messy hair
words impaired
people will turn on you in a beat
so, move along and pounce your feet
before they call on someone to take you off the street

norm. (40)

coloring within the lines
will be just fine
but, you'll never know
what it's like to exist in the afterglow
of breaking the rules
that weren't right for you

secrets. (102)

secrets we keep
way down beneath
will someday get out
and, others will doubt
what they knew of you
and, there may be a bitter feud
but, you are what you are
you just have to accept the cards

no gf. (148)

what say you, young man?
not much
no plan
you play it by ear
you hide your fear
born in the wrong year

funds. (111)

there's no better scare
than looking at what's accumulated
or, rather what's not there

like them. (28)

you worked so hard to be like them
you dressed the part and stay open
to the many things that just don't fit
saw yourself become a hypocrite
so, you walked away and became legit

indemnified. (66)

not everything is so black and white
we each have contributed to the plight
of our humanity
society
civility
so, don't walk away thinking you had no part
in the hot mess that has been building so far

insta vs. reality. (24)

a baby coos in the nursery room
a mother longs to escape real soon

fans in the arena screaming his name
the artist sits in a hotel room going insane

a beautiful bride walks down the aisle
the groom wonders whether it's all worthwhile

a father receives accolades for his life's work
a son waddles in a dope-filled murk

cancel. (161)

we lived during the reign of giants
worshipped at their feet
spoke their stories with reverence
and, rarely thought about what lie beneath

now, fast forward to today
we demand perfection and nothing less
when their curtains are ripped open
we are appalled at the ugly mess

we then cast them out from existence
because we can't tolerate the truth
that these giants were imposters
and, were really just like me and you

sleep. (63)

let go
close eyes
breathe
synchronize
heart beats
tingle
mind flees
detangle
forget the past
enter the abyss
don't look back

masses. (131)

lemmings, we be
original thoughts, a scarcity
the herd, we join happily
our future, sacrificed easily

grey. (71)

when will we learn
that absolutes don't exist
that as this world turns
a blend will persist
for on paper, i am with you
though sometimes i agree with the other dude
i just don't speak so
afraid it might affect the flow

but shouldn't we just be okay?
with coloring outside the lines
instead of keeping ourselves at bay

main street i. (99)

people just want to be
happier than what's reality

be true. (95)

this is our lot in life
the churn
the burn
the limited sight
no chance at a different plight

our paths were paved long ago
yet, we continue to believe
there's flexibility
in our finale

so, we deny the truth
of what we were meant to be
a loss for us
and this world, ultimately

apathy. (45)

i would like to accentuate
the need for us to participate
for things won't move along
unless we sing the age-old song

antagonists. (105)

this world is full of cocks
who will want to drive you nuts

pay them no mind
gravitate towards the kind

familial. (168)

the noise your loved ones make
can sometimes be a comfort to one's heart
an assurance you're not alone
yet, can also be an obligatory part

nor black, nor white. (123)

not every pauper has a heart of gold
not every miser is an asshole
some people deserve a second chance
others will keep sinning
no matter the number of allowances

it's all a gamble in the end
we all know that the house usually wins
but, every once in a while, the odds take a spin
and, we will see an upside once again

why you. (121)

no one said it would be easy
let alone a guarantee
but, when things don't go your way
you sulk and begin to decay

get up and don't look back!
because all that matters
is how you react

border. (97)

oh, yeah
we're going to regret
this heinous act we've committed
our compassion has slacked

you ii. (6b)

what can i say about you?
the one who speaks no truth
you tell great tales
your work prevails
you'll falter one day soon

what can i say about you?
the one with red-soled shoes
you paid with debt
and i wanna bet
there are many more IOUs

what can i say about you?
the one who pushes through
your ruthless side
is no source of pride
hope you'll step in some poo

the standard. (74)

i thought about
our words and pout
and you know what?
it doesn't matter much

we sit here and critique from afar
with little regard
for those who actually take up a cause

we demand perfection
of those who bear the cross
yet, we ourselves rarely reach excellence
and, we typically realize less wins than loss

when will we wake up and look within?
for then we will see that we are not without sin
but, persevering despite our flaws
is what will make us better people overall

don't stay. (137)

i once felt a tremor
beneath my bare feet
i know i should've fled
but, i had see what could be
little did i know this would be my end
and, now i wish i would've been open
to being one with less curiosity

main street ii. (108)

just do me this favor
get to know your neighbor
it will pay off later

every life. (132)

breathe in and out
don't think about the doubt
it will be over by sundown
then freedom will be your shout
until the next morning
when you will need to breathe in and out

noel. (78)

it's that time of year
when we all give good cheer
and, all that pains disappears
and, we hope and pray
that the next days
will be a better place
than what we've had to face

out of the woods. (152)

there is still hope
for those of us who dream the most
we just need to find a clear path from here
to avoid the wild and associated fear
but, it is up to us to take the step
forward towards an evolved depth
for if we don't move fast
we'll quickly be sucked into the past

understand. (162)

we're lacking one critical component
empathy is what it's called
we can't move forward without it
it must be the crux of it all

once we are able to look at each other
read one another's souls
then the healing will begin
and, we will reach our ultimate goal

work. (170)

weekends are meant for reflection
a moment from all that's disruptive
in a life that runs 100 miles a minute
and, doesn't result in productive

generations. (171)

the youth of today are no different
than the ones that preceded in years
the tone has become somewhat belligerent
but, the message is the same to old ears

all for one. (174)

it will only work
if you open doors
for those who look to challenge
your approach and talent

wake up. (114)

they don't really care
about your problems
yet, you continue to stand there
seeking solace

when will you see
you poor, insecure plebe
they're using you
and, you'll never be free

establishment

you iii. (82)

your narcissism can drain me
i'm not in the mood to constantly be
in your service day and night
because i have to think about other delights

so, what about moving along?
just for a minute or maybe for long

i'll miss you, don't worry
but, here's your bag and hurry

accept it. (59)

hi, ho
you say,
what the hell is going on
why folks so scorned

i say,
all this time you've been blind
to the sounds of the other kind
you patronized them
did the minimum
to silence the forgotten
but, it didn't work bro
they've been secretly waiting for an overthrow
and, now the time is here
no turning back to the prior years
you've got to deal with it now
yours to win or foul

disappoint. (87)

the shame you bring
to our family and soil
you continue to sing
and, you continue to toil
towards the decay
of what we've built
so, we're waiting for the day
when you finally feel the guilt

wolf. (49)

you sing in unison with the choir
when alone, your tune becomes fire
when exposed, you deny being a brute
but, we all know the truth
you know what you are
so, go work on yourself, preferably somewhere far

jefe. (145)

let's get this straight
you're hiding from your destiny
it's not up for debate
stand up
speak up
give a damn much?

why are you here?
if you can't sit up and commandeer

liar. (70)

you've got to be kidding me
i know you're lying
and, you assume others didn't see
but, i sensed your stink
once you entered my door
and, you think
i'm gonna fall for your lore
out of here
your presence disgusts me
and, stay away
we don't need your cray

self aware. (44)

you have no idea who you are
but, you want to be a star
you are quite a narcissist
yet, want to be thought as benevolent
and, wonder why others don't see
what you think you are to be

for real. (84)

the things you say
to keep non-believers at bay
and, the truth away

for if we knew you for real
you think you might not appeal
to those whose favor you desire
but, you know, they're also liars

stink. (124)

you remind me of what i don't want to be
the hate, the ignorance and audacity
that, one day, will do you in
but, i'm guessing you don't give a shit
so, i've gotta be your opposite
to make sure, in the end
the good guys end up with a win

false prophet. (25)

you've pumped us up with your passionate sermon
about how we should be determined
to demand coin, title and station
to speak up without trepidation

your message was copyrighted
and, read by generations who'd been slighted
making promises about how everything should fall in
place
once we follow your steps in this exhausting rat race

millions began seeing you as the holy mater
who could deliver us from this world of violators
but, then scandal hit
and, so you hid
no leadership to give
even though your sole purpose was to be supportive

being on top is not always a breeze
which is something you should've shared with your
devotees
in all your time spreading the word
you should've mentioned that falling on your sword
is sometimes an important part of leading the herd

it's time. (80)

you've had a good run
now's the time to give it up
let a prodigy give it a try
while you're still around to share insight

hypocrite. (75)

i'm going to sell you a future
that promises to be purer
than what we've been witnessing
from ojai to flushing

now, i'll leave out some details
about how my ancestors set sail
because if you heard the story
you'd get rid of me in a hurry

look & listen. (55)

i scream out loud
yet, you don't seem to hear me
much less
see me
you're blind
to what's beyond your front yard
i warn you now
the day will come
when a reckoning will happen
and, then you will hear and see
and, you won't be able
to ignore the plea

bad boy. (92)

i don't have patience
for your manipulation

you're in the wrong
yet, take no fault
and, you use your position
to influence the decision

may you one day reap
what you have seeded

not equal. (94)

you expect me to fawn over you
stroke your ego
giggle at a few
but, don't you see
i don't need you
as you need me
so, how about spinning this around
and, showing me how
you're worthy now

racist. (119)

you are what you are
your denials aren't genuine
you know what you think
you just don't want the world to see you're a bigot
so, you'll keep on denying
while we see right through your lying

dumb dumb. (146)

boy, you don't know much
yet, you're living your best life now
now, that's fucked up

public safety. (153)

yeah
our roads will diverge much more
i had hoped we could find some rapport
but, your asinine ways
may bring the end of days

no speako ingles. (68)

aquí no podemos usar
las palabras que no son american
el gringo tiene miedo
so, make sure you go
home and speak quietly
and, hope no one enters unexpectedly
to take you back from whence you came
a un país que no te quiere también

finally. (185)

the sleepers been woken
the people have spoken
in the currency that matters
so, it's time for these servants to scatter

though, we must use this time wisely
to find ways to unite, please
because we can't regress again
to a place where facts don't win

index

about the poet

This is **M.E.** Lanie's first collection of published poems. She currently lives in Florida. To learn more about **M.E.** Lanie, you can follow her on Facebook, Twitter, or Instagram - @laniepoetry.